Democratic Thinking
and the War

Democratic Thinking and the War

THE WILLIAM H. WHITE LECTURES

AT THE UNIVERSITY OF VIRGINIA

[1942–1943]

By Francis Biddle

ATTORNEY GENERAL

OF THE UNITED STATES

Charles Scribner's Sons

NEW YORK · 1944

THIS BOOK IS
MANUFACTURED UNDER WARTIME
CONDITIONS IN CONFORMITY WITH
ALL GOVERNMENT REGULATIONS
CONTROLLING THE USE OF PAPER
AND OTHER MATERIALS

For Randolph
From His Father

AUTHOR'S NOTE

One of the penalties for writing about current affairs is the rapidity with which those affairs change. In reading the proofs of these lectures, delivered a year and six months ago, I realize that I must suffer this penalty in aggravated form. For, in the period that has intervened, the atmosphere with respect to foreign affairs has changed very markedly and public opinion as a whole has kept pace with the march of events. By the same token, the tension between the Congress and the Executive Branch—the subject of the second lecture—has very considerably relaxed. But the underlying problems—with which the lectures are principally concerned—remain very much the same. This, I trust, is sufficient justification for permitting their publication now.

F. B.

Washington, D. C.
December 4, 1943

THE WILLIAM H. WHITE FOUNDATION

This Foundation was established in 1922, a gift of Mrs. Emma Gray White, widow, Mrs. Emma Gray Trigg, daughter, and W. H. Landon White and William H. White, Jr., sons, of the late William H. White, a distinguished alumnus and for many years a Visitor of the University of Virginia. The conditions require that the income be used in securing each session the delivery before the University Law School of a series of lectures, preferably not less than three in number, by a jurist or publicist who is specially distinguished in some branch of jurisprudence, domestic, international or foreign; and that the lecturer present some fresh or unfamiliar aspect of his subject. Each series of lectures shall possess such unity that they may be published in book form.

PART ONE

*Notes on
Democratic Thinking*

Notes on
*Democratic Thinking**

I SHOULD not pause in the work of the war—or permit myself to tempt you to do so—were not the moment propitious for introspection. The progress of our arms drives home more clearly with each passing day the world-wide implications of the task to which we have devoted our country and our lives. What we do or fail to do, what we seek or fail to seek, what we think or fail to think—has potent meaning not alone for ourselves but for the humblest spirit anywhere on the face of the earth. Men have spoken glibly of the future of the world. Not even the hardiest cynic will smile when I say now—in the most measured terms—that its future depends upon ourselves—upon the force and the imagination, upon the intellect and the passion of the democracy we call our own. I repeat, therefore, that the time is appropriate for introspection; and to us who believe in democracy, who are the bearers of the democratic

---

*Lecture delivered before the Law School of the University of Virginia, December 4, 1942.

3

message, for better or for worse, to all the peoples of the earth, it is a time for democratic introspection. If the time is correct, so without a doubt is the place. You who live and work almost within sight of Monticello know that here the very air and shadows keep watch for our democracy—here where so much of the democratic hope was born, where so much of its creed was written.

Unless I mistake the lesson of events, what we think about ourselves determines in the long run what we are and what we are capable of doing. Hence my concern in this paper is less with what democracy is than what we, its citizens and workers in its cause, think it is. I shall, in short, forsake a single thesis and read you my note-book on a variety of themes, basic, it seems to me, in the current of democratic thought.

I

It has been said, and often with some heat, that we are derelict in our duty in failing to state the ends for which we fight this war. Those who voice the criticism confound the statement of our ends with a catalogue of available means.

Our immediate end in fighting this war is to win both the war and the peace that is to come. For as the President said on October 12, 1942, it "is useless to win a war unless it stays won. . . . We are united in seeking the kind of victory that will guarantee that our grandchildren can grow and, under God, may live their lives, free from the constant threat of invasion, destruction, slavery and violent death." This we seek for ourselves, the chance to develop our democracy in our own way, free from external restraint.

What we seek for others was stated by the President and Winston Churchill in August of 1941. As unequivocally as words can tell, they said: "Their countries seek no aggrandizement . . . desire to see no territorial changes that do not accord with the freely expressed wishes of the peoples concerned . . . respect the right of all peoples to choose the form of government under which they will live . . . [with] sovereign rights and self-government restored." Nor did the Atlantic Charter, so-called may I remind you from the place where it was written rather than the subject with which it deals, stop with a guaranty of political integrity. Access to trade and raw materials, improved labor standards, economic advancement and social security were among the "common principles." Freedom of the seas, abandonment of the

5

use of force, and, correlatively, the establishment of a permanent system of general security are among the stated aims. When to these are added the President's emphasis on the four freedoms everywhere, it is difficult to see how democratic hopes and democratic faith could be articulated in plainer terms. The two phases of our heritage of freedom have here been brought together: the first and the older phase, the protection of individual men and women against tyrants and the tyrant state; the second and newer phase, the protection of individual men and women against what Senator Wagner has called "social and economic conditions in which human beings cannot be free." Projected on the plane of the future, extended to all the corners of the earth, these are our ultimate hopes, the ends for which we fight.

It is in the nature of these hopes that while they add much to the force of our arms many of them cannot be realized by the force of arms alone. The force that holds men in bondage can be broken by superior force; the starvation that makes them slaves can be dissipated by giving them food; the ignorance that binds them to earth can be dispelled by the knowledge that points to the stars. But what men do with freedom depends in the end upon themselves.

The point is the old one, often repeated by Justice Brandeis, with reference to our problems at home. "Democracy," he once said, "is a serious undertaking which substitutes self-restraint for external restraint." Thus, as he told the Commission on Industrial Relations in 1914, speaking of the relation of management and labor, "however much we may desire material improvement and must desire it for the comfort of the individual, the United States is a democracy and we must have, above all things, men. . . . The social justice for which we are striving is an incident to our democracy, not the main end. It is rather the result of democracy—perhaps its finest expression—but it rests upon democracy—which implies rule by the people." His concern over the growth of huge corporations sprang, as all men know, from the fear that the exercise of their power would paralyze individual initiative and thus impair creative strength. And his belief in preserving the fundamental rights protected by the first ten Amendments arose from the judgment, so clearly made by the Founders, that they are essential constituents of "a free climate for individual men."

To accept these views is but to say that the democracy which is our concern at home and abroad is at bottom a concern for individual human beings.

It is upon them that we must depend for the fruition of our hopes; it is for them that the hopes are dear. Men cannot be made by having the state give them their ideas, choose their leaders, provide their religion. Government, however efficient, is not an end but a means. The people are the end, the men and women who make their governments to suit their lives. Thought of as an end, set free of the needs of the human beings it is intended to serve, government, turning mechanical, must become either impotent or brutal. Institutions cannot be given a life of their own, divorced from the flesh and blood of men. The inevitable result, when such distortion occurs, is summarized in the dogmas of the totalitarian state.

This bold democratic faith is affirmed not only by liberals but by groups that we think of as properly conservative. A "blue print" for the post-war world was drawn in September, 1942, at the Inter-American Seminar on social studies called by the National Catholic Welfare Conference. Condemning totalitarianism, calling for the establishment of "a just and free order for all the peoples," the statement speaks of the necessity "to make economic life serve the general good of all mankind" through the free organization of business, labor, farmers and the professions, assisted and supervised by government. Implicit in the statement is the insistence that the rights of men must be further protected and enhanced. "The crisis of our civilization . . . springs from a false notion of man. . . . Political systems and philosophical systems that deny the equality of mankind and break its unity, the lust for domination and the persecutions founded on racial and religious discrimination are inhuman, anti-Christian and barbarous." The preservation and exercise of individual rights, the Seminar holds, should "obtain recognition and protection in every social order. . . . Democracy, whatever its deficiencies may have been in the past, is certainly opposed to Totalitarianism, and when it is directed by Christian principles constitutes a system under which Christian living can best be achieved. . . . Social reform is necessary immediately. . . . The working people must get their just wage. . . . They must have economic security. . . . Access to ownership . . . must be broadened as widely as possible. Free organization of labor must be guaranteed. . . . The poor must live well. . . . The purpose and justification of the war is not vengeance but the establishment of a just and free order for all the peoples of the world." All this is implicit in the Atlantic Charter and the authoritative statements of

9

our ends that have already been made. Those who do not find it there have not yet learned to read.

II

What I have said comes then to this: It is democracy for which we fight this war—its preservation and enrichment for ourselves and its extension, so far as possible, to those to whom it is now denied. I have no doubt that it is this faith in a democratic future that stirs in England, in China, and in Russia, in the hearts of our soldiers in the field and of the soldiers of our Allies. But, I have asked myself, is that what we *really* think—we, the people of America who are here and still at home? Is our spirit genuinely moved by the vision of a better world or do we shrink from the future, disturbed by anxiety about increased taxation and the threat of unemployment after the war? Do the people of our land fight only to win the war and have it over—or to use the war for great and democratic ends?

In a recent lecture delivered in England Mr. Archibald MacLeish has addressed himself to these questions with his usual eloquence. Speaking of the period following our initial defensive reaction to Pearl Harbor, he said:

There was something new now in the world, something forward in time, and the people felt it. They recognized it in each others' faces, in each others' courage, in the newspaper accounts of the resistance of the people elsewhere, in the radio stories from the many fronts. They knew that the President was right when he told them that the militarists of Rome and Tokyo and Berlin had begun this war, but that they would end it—that the people would end it. They propose to end it and to end it, not by defeating the purpose of the enemies of the people only, but by realizing a purpose of their own—a clear and forming purpose—a purpose to live like men, to live with dignity and in freedom, and like men.

Often enough a poet's insight yields the truest measure of the facts. But if this sense of democratic purpose has, as I trust, become the spirit of our people as a whole, it is barely revealed in the pages of the daily press. A study of 125 newspapers during the months of August and September suggests a picture far less clear. The apathy in some quarters concerning post-war aims seems compatible only with lack of interest. Some commentators, to be sure, have suggested rather vaguely that we must plan for after the war—but in the ultimate impact of the press their voices do not predominate over the contrary view that consideration of the future is likely to detract from the war effort, and being necessarily visionary

11

may endanger the system of private enterprise. The thought is not limited to the press. Keep your eyes on the ground!

When I speak of post-war aims, I am not, of course, referring to detailed terms of peace. I refer to the underlying spirit, the general principles in terms of which details will be appraised. These are the very spirit of the war itself; they must necessarily become part of our lives. If we bury our heads in the sand until the martial winds have passed, we shall not raise them at the end with vision unimpaired. Speaking in Boston on October 8, 1942, the Under-Secretary of State, Mr. Sumner Welles, made emphatically clear that the Administration is no party to the discouragement of constructive thought. "One hears it said," he observed, "that no thought should be given to the problems of the peace, nor to the problems of the transitional period between war and established peace, until after the war has been won. The shallowness of such thinking, whether sincere or sinister, is apparent."

For most of the purposes of thought there is in truth no sharp break between the peace and the war. In the continuum of time and history a new order does not emerge from a picture book; it is necessarily a part of what has gone before. In that sense the peace is a part of the war, just as the war was fed by the failures of the unsolid peace that ended the last great war. Yesterday Pearl Harbor, and with the treacherous attack the end of divergence and doubt. Today North Africa with its face turned toward tomorrow in Southern Europe, the next sure step. The force of arms and the establishment of order shortly to be followed by the patient work of relief and rehabilitation. Even while the soldier stands guard, the doctor, the engineer, the relief worker will point to the tasks of peace, releasing as they work the pent constructive energy of newly liberated lands. Compartmentalized thinking about war and peace will not keep pace with the march of such events. Ancient fears of entangling alliances, the traditional instinct to view the problems of the Old World as essentially dissimilar from our own will be unable to compete with the pressing realities of hope and need that will accompany and follow the war.

III

If, as Mr. MacLeish has said, "there is something new now in the world," I believe that it is the sensed chance and the formed will to view the long future in the largest democratic terms. What this may mean concretely—whether at home or abroad—we cannot yet foretell. Clarity on ends does not produce an equal clarity on means. But I can illustrate the challenge we must face at home by figures close at hand. Alvin H. Hansen and Guy Greer tell us in a recent article in *Fortune* that in 1941, when there was already a very large output of armaments, consumers' expenditures in the United States for privately produced goods and services was $75,800,000,000 as compared with $70,800,000,000 in 1929, the great boom year; and that after allowing for price changes and increase in population "the amount available per capita for consumption was about 10 per cent higher than in 1929." The gross national product for 1943 was estimated at 165 billions, against 100 billions in 1929. How shall we read such statements? Shall we take them as a prophecy of doom after the war is won or as a promise of a peace economy geared to similar productive proportions, its potentialities almost unimaginable for the satisfaction of consumers' needs? Those who grasp the breadth of democratic aspiration will certainly see a promise and not a doom.

This is not to say that there are no difficulties in the road ahead or that we can underestimate what difficulties there are. Some of them, indeed, involve

14

recurrent issues in the patterns of democratic thinking. To state them now may, at the least, assist us in appraising their scope.

There is, first, the fear of change and with it the failure to realize that while the democratic purpose is constant the special functions of democracy are constantly being transformed. Where once men fought to protect themselves against Star Chamber, to be represented if they were taxed, to hold their own religion or resist one foisted on them by the state, so they fought another day to protect themselves against exploitation by industry and finance. Yet such change, destructive as it may be to accustomed ways of thinking, is of the essence of a democratic life. If, as I have said, democracy is ultimately rooted in a positive demand for a broader distribution of individual happiness; if, as I believe, the democratic urge springs from the insistence on life as an end in itself as opposed to the negation of state-worship—then change is the breath of its nostrils, growth and variety its welcome resources. Democracy can be no more static than life. It must move and grow in order to endure at all. This, if anything, we have learned in the years that have passed. We shall need to believe it firmly in the years that will come.

I have spoken of the fear of change; along with it is the fear of planning. Some among us tremble at the word, sensing a regimentation foreign to our fundamental concepts. Yet we have always planned —Franklin and Hamilton, Webster and Clay. What, indeed, has had a greater power to stir the national spirit than plans, clearly formulated and honestly expressed, pointing the promise of our democratic hopes? Yet you must have heard, as I have, the shudders that accompany mention of a "planned economy," followed as they always are by whispers of "socialism" and the destruction of the American System. The truth is that all economy is planned, as is successful business enterprise or any other form of intelligent life. For planning is nothing more nor less than an attempt to face problems and to solve them. The important question you may be sure is not whether there will be planning—there is bound to be so long as people think—but who is to make the plans and what they will be like. What is important to the people of a democracy is that the plans that are made promote their interests and that they have a part in their formulation and execution. But unless wise planning occurs it is democracy itself that will ultimately be set adrift.

The third difficulty I would mention I shall call

the difficulty of the oversimplified choice. We have encountered it often in the past as the choice between communism and fascism, or again, between *laissez-faire* and benevolent socialism, or still again, between not enough food and too much state. In times of economic stress, or overrapid social organization, there is a tendency to set up the nonexistent dilemmas posed by such absolutistic choice. Often enough the exponents of government control tend in this way to put all their eggs in a single basket, forgetting that human strength and cohesion can frequently express themselves in the natural groupings of self-interest moving behind the cloak of government more naturally than through the government itself. By the same token, the opposing school, viewing with alarm a law which impinges on their interests, yields readily to articulate horror at what it asserts to be the approach of totalitarian rule. What is overlooked in such overdrawn conclusions, is that government, with its rôle reasonably defined in relation to the facts of human living, is not incompatible with a just society, anymore than a country reasonably free from those who govern it is incompatible with one that is also reasonably free from want. To put the matter in another way, the fault with such dilemmas is that they overlook the basic assumption of any democratic society, the assumption of compromise. If, as has been said, life is but a compromise with our environment, how can its political expression avoid an entirely comparable pattern? Were not life the give and take that it is, necessarily imperfect in any abstract terms, there would be no need for government at all. What is, in the end, of the essence of dictatorship and of the spirit of those who could accept it, is the insistence on one set of ideas, formulated from one source of power, controlling all alike. Such insistence and nothing more is involved in these absolutes of choice.

A fourth difficulty, closely related to that of the oversimplified choice, is the notion of a rigid distinction between the function of the Government and the function of private enterprise. This, indeed, has been the central theme of our political controversies for half a hundred years. I do not deny that uppermost in the minds of the Founders was the concept of a limited government, limited by inherent weakness as well as by law. They were determined to prevent the abuses of power which they had experienced in dealing with George the Third. The less government, they thought, the better. Yet this intended weakness, designed to strengthen the individual, speedily threatened to sanction his destruction at the hands of enterprise itself. So it was that the powers of unregulated business had to be checked by transferring much of their control from private to public hands. The shift occurred not under pressure of theory but in response to practical need. Where theory pointed to the *status quo* of governmental negativity, shippers and tradesmen, farmers and consumers and finally labor as well insisted on redressing the balance that theory would have denied. This is familiar history, to be sure, but it is history that we must constantly keep in mind.

It is this history that is denied by such assertions as that made a few years ago by a former president of the United States Chamber of Commerce when it had become clear that the New Deal did not intend to confine itself to saving the railroads and the banks: "The best public servant," he said, "is the worst one. . . . A thoroughly first-class man in public service is corrosive. He eats holes in our liberties. The better he is and the longer he stays the greater is the danger." It is the same history that is denied when, about two years ago, the chairman of the Board of Directors of one of our greatest industrial giants published as a full-time advertisement in the *Saturday Evening Post* what he was pleased to call "An American Primer." There were seven "items" of the interesting declaration, "set down," as the distinguished executive expressed it, "in simple language." "Remember," the second item ran, "that government belongs to the people, is inherently inefficient, and that its activity should be limited to those which government alone can perform."

It is not the past alone that is denied when, as I read on November 17, 1942, the President of the National Association of Manufacturers asserted that the task of industry is to prevent "the continuance of Government control after the war" because "the time will come when patriotism is no longer stimulated by the present emotional impulses"; or when the governor of a great state suggested, if the New York *Times* is to be believed, that the nation is in greater danger of losing its democracy through the expansion of Federal bureaus than through a military defeat. I suppose that there are men who, reading such stuff at breakfast, nod over their orange juice and say to their wives, "By George, he's right. That's sound stuff." But is it a contribution to the solution of the problems we face?

You will not think, because I have used strong words, that I ignore or underestimate the danger that governmental powers may be abused. My point is, rather, that the problem of the overconcentration and the misuse of power involves government and enterprise alike; corporate organizations, labor monopolies—any other grouping of human beings—may acquire more power than they should have or may use such power as they have for purposes inimical to the general good. The misuse of power is neither more likely nor more necessarily harmful in the case of the government than it is in the case of the other social organisms where power has been or may be lodged. Yet as Mr. Ordway Tead observed in September, 1942, in a penetrating article in the *Survey Graphic* called "Life, Liberty and the Pursuit of Power": "It is worth noting that no one has ever seriously proposed that business corporations be run on a two-party system. The government system of checks and balances would be felt by practical business administrators and by experts in the principles of business administration to be a completely archaic and haywire way to proceed." I have no doubt that the many business men now participating in government would heartily endorse this view.

By the same token and on the other side it will no more do to think of the state as necessarily coercive than to think of enterprise as necessarily free. There is, as Lewis Mumford has said, an important difference between the power and the service state, a difference which led him to write that "the real alternative to the empty political patterns of the nineteenth century lies not in totalitarianism, but in just the opposite of this: the restoration of the human scale in government, the multiplication of the units of autonomous service, the widening of the cooperative processes of government, the general reduction of the area of arbitrary compulsion, the restoration of the processes of persuasion and rational agreement."

What is important in considering the allocation of power between government and private groups is, therefore, a sober appraisal of the potentialities and the effectiveness of each, in the context of the particular job to be done. It is relevant to such an appraisal that business management, however much in our day it has been divorced from ownership and become a type of self-perpetuating control, is essentially stable and continuing, and that it may be capable of efficiencies that government is hard put to provide. It is equally relevant that government, being, as has been said, "the largest club to which we all belong," is responsive, and necessarily must be, to the popular will, at the same time that it is capable of marshalling human and material resources that no private agency can supply.

To define the role of democratic government in

positive terms is, of course, to imply the necessity of trained and competent personnel. Long ago Mr. Bryce in his *American Commonwealth* asserted that we have a tendency to belittle our heroes in public life (especially, I suggest, if they are contemporary), a trait which he connected with the admirable virtue of self-confidence. After allowing for what he called the "humorous tendencies of the American mind" he suggested that "the fact remains that, although no people is more emotional, and even in a sense more poetical, in no country is the ideal side of public life, what one may venture to call the heroic element in a public career, so ignored by the mass and repudiated by the leaders. This affects not only the elevation but the independence and courage of public men; and the country suffers from the want of what we call distinction in its conspicuous figures." I doubt that this appraisal was generally accurate when it was written. Though it is reflected today in occasional statements, such as those I have quoted, it is certainly not now true to the facts. But it suggests the more genuine difficulty, expressed by A. Lawrence Lowell when he was teaching government many years ago, that the test of democracy is its ability to use experts. The average American nurses a suspicion of the expert function in government, a suspicion frequently exploited for merely political ends.

The suspicion is a healthy one to be sure and it rests on a shrewd instinct. The instinct is manifested by our legal tradition in the use of the jury to counterbalance the specialist judge—the characteristic genius of the common law to develop human correctives against its own instruments of justice. By entrusting the final decision to ordinary folks we "let a little popular prejudice into the administration of law" (as Justice Holmes suggested to Lady Pollock), and thus assure that judges and lawyers keep at least one foot on the ground. So it may be noted on a larger plane that government, being hardly an art and certainly not a science, must rely on common wisdom rather than on special skill. The underlying issues, involving matters of broad policy, call for a balancing of values as varied as the national life itself. The expert, being by definition a man who knows a great deal about a particular subject, has no special competence to make such decisions; they must be made by laymen and they are.

But that is not to say that the layman can function in the intricate ramifications of modern government without the aid of the expert, or, indeed, of a corps of experts to deal with the special problems that arise. Data must be assembled and interpreted; technical questions must be stated and explored. Unless this is done the ultimate issues to be resolved by laymen will but rarely be brought to hand. Moreover, administration has more and more become a technical enterprise requiring expert skill for the effectuation of whatever policy is authoritatively made. Thus, without special competence at the service of government, democratic choice would have difficulty in reaching decision, and the decision when taken would rarely be put in force. Civil Service and the improvement of merit systems are, in this context, promising developments, tending to raise the quality of the public service without perpetuating the policy makers who must change with a new administration and even with shifts in points of view as a single administration proceeds. Properly administered this framework can meet the double necessity of new blood in public office and the continuity of trained personnel. But the problem is far from solved. It will not be solved unless the country recognizes that the danger for the future is not that the experts will pre-empt the powers of government but, rather, that democratic government will be unable to utilize as much expertness as it needs.

IV

I have spoken of democratic purposes and of some of the difficulties that must be overcome in our own thinking if such purposes are to be genuinely achieved. What in the end will sweep the difficulties away is the tenacity of the democratic hope itself. We shall not return from great work and high adventure abroad and be content with small accomplishments here. When we have seen, in the mirror of war, what organized effort can achieve, we shall not be content, facing the peace, with the unrealistic compromises that played so large a part in bringing about this crisis in the history of democratic development.

PART TWO

*The Government
and the War*

The Government
and the War*

IN MY first lecture I spoke of the democratic ends for which we fight this war and some of the traditional difficulties which must be overcome in our own thinking if democratic purposes are to be genuinely achieved. I pointed to the fear of change and the horror of planning, the tendency to view complex problems in terms of such oversimplified dilemmas as the choice between socialism and *laissez-faire;* the assumption of a rigid distinction between the functions of government and of private enterprise, with government inevitably evil and enterprise necessarily good; the suspicion of experts in government as an abiding threat to popular rule. These are difficulties which go not merely to the structure of government—the distribution of power among the various branches of the Federal Government and between the nation and the states; they go to the entire governmental enterprise and thus de-

*Lecture delivered before the Law School of the University of Virginia, May 3, 1943.

termine in the largest sense the measure of our aspirations and our powers. Speaking in December, it seemed appropriate to state our essential problems in such general and long-range terms. You will understand why it is that speaking in May I intend to concern myself with recent developments and to outline our difficulties in much more immediate terms.

I

The five months that have passed since I first addressed you have been months of unmistakable reaction. This is not surprising in view of what has been accomplished and the sacrifices that grow increasingly necessary as the war program proceeds. That the reaction should have become swiftly articulate following an election which resulted in gains to the opponents of the Administration was to be expected. Its manifestation in Congress has, of course, taken the form of an attack upon the Executive Branch of the Government, the powers under which it operates, the appropriations by which it functions and its extensive civilian personnel. The lawmakers, having vested the broadest powers in the President to supplement his Constitutional authority as Commander in Chief, having directed the Executive to act promptly and vigorously, now protest the exercise of delegated powers by challenging the necessity for having delegated them at all. The attack transcends particular acts of alleged maladministration and includes the field of administration as a whole. Administrators, whether old-line civil servants, New Deal administrators or business men employed in the new war agencies, are grouped as "bureaucrats"; and the legislators appear as popular champions, struggling to win back for the people the powers which the "bureaucrats" have usurped. Administration is discussed as if it were essentially incompatible with legislation, and the attack on administrative agencies gathers new life. Even some of the friends of the New Deal program, giving voice to the popular sentiment, hit the new sawdust trail which leads to casting out the "bureaucrats" from the body politic.

This climate of opinion manifested in daily discussion on the floor of Congress as well as in action on specific measures, was given its most pointed expression in the mounting enthusiasm to investigate the Executive Branch and all its works. The standing committees of the House and Senate, including the great committees on appropriations, are the traditional media through which the Congress maintains

31

its necessary critical awareness of the details of administrative operations. A number of special committees were, in addition, functioning at the close of the last session, notably the Truman Committee established to investigate the National Defense Program, and the Joint Committee on Reduction of Non-Essential Federal Expenditures. A score of resolutions introduced at the present session in the House and more than a dozen in the Senate proposed to add to the normal work of the established committees special investigations into various aspects of the work of the Executive Branch. Many of the proposals, particularly in the House, were for the creation of special committees.

By the middle of March, the House, in addition to continuing the Dies Committee and the Committee on Small Business had by resolution authorized the Committees on Military and Naval Affairs to investigate the progress of the war effort; it had empowered the Civil Service Committee "to conduct thorough studies and investigation of the policies and practices relating to civilian employment in the departments and agencies of the Government, including government-owned corporations"; it had created a Select Committee to investigate the organization, personnel, and activities of the Federal Communications Commission to determine whether the Commission is "acting in accordance with law and the public interest"; it had established a Select Committee to investigate the Farm Security Administration (which it subsequently voted to destroy) "with a view to determining whether or not such activities are being carried on in accordance with the policies of Congress expressed in the laws"; it had authorized the Committee on Public Buildings and Grounds to conduct an investigation into the progress of the entire defense housing program; it had directed the Committee on Appropriations, through a subcommittee, to examine charges that certain persons in the employ of the executive agencies are unfit for public employment because of association with subversive organizations; it had granted general authority to the Committee on Appropriations "to conduct such studies and examination of the organization and operation of any executive department or . . . agency . . . as the Committee may deem necessary to assist it in connection with the determination of matters within its jurisdiction"; and, finally, it had established a special committee "to conduct investigations of any action, rule, procedure, regulation, order or directive taken or promulgated by any department or independent agency of the Federal Government

33

where complaint is made" to the committee that the action deprives citizens of Constitutional rights, or otherwise exceeds the agency's power or inflicts a penalty without affording an opportunity to present a defense "before a fair and impartial tribunal."

I cite this enumeration not in criticism of the House or any of the committees, but rather to exhibit the temper of the Congress with respect to the Executive Branch after seventeen months of war. There is hardly a field of executive action that is not being critically reviewed—often by several committees in succession or even at the same time.

At least one member of the House, Representative Dirksen of Illinois, has made clear that he regards it as appropriate for Congress not only to investigate the executive agencies as the occasion arises but to maintain a day by day review of their activities in the exercise of their rule-making authority. On January 25 Mr. Dirksen introduced a resolution—thus far not adopted—proposing to establish a Joint Committee on Administrative Review to which all agencies would be required to submit their rules and regulations before they could become effective. Within ten days the committee would determine whether the rule submitted runs "counter to the intent of Congress in creating and delegating the functions for the enforcement of which it is proposed." If the agency is notified that the proposed rule does violate the intent of Congress as construed by the committee, the rule could not be made effective until the expiration of forty days. Even if Congress took no adverse action during the forty-day period, it may be assumed that the objection of the committee would in normal circumstances have the force of a moral veto.

Mr. Dirksen fully recognizes that implementation of his plan would necessitate the establishment, under the ægis of the committee, of a corps of Congressional experts to study what the administrators propose to do. He has in mind that the committee will actually police administrative procedures. This is indicated by his comments on the resolution. "There must be bureaucratic discipline," he said; ". . . there should be review. I am persuaded that a great many bungling procedures of the Office of Price Administration, a great many of the severities in the rationing program could have been avoided if a group of legislators could sit down with a staff and examine them meticulously and straighten them out and send them back and say, 'With these modifications they are all right.' So we need *legislative review*."

II

To what extent this suspicion of the Executive Branch is reflected in prevailing public sentiment, I shall not undertake to judge. It is, to be sure, one of the great functions of Congress to act, as it has been said, as "an organ of registration, an instrument of criticism, a sounding board through which the voice of the nation can make itself heard." Congress is the immediate link between the people and their ser-vants in the Executive Branch, the ever-present guar-antee that administration will remain reasonably close to the line of popular will. It is extraordinary how fast the irritations of private citizens over what they believe to be unnecessary or unfair in govern-ment are translated into Congressional criticism of administration. What begins in specific complaints soon swells into attacks on policy. A member of Congress, finding himself often enough the unhappy victim of an enraged constituent's dissatisfaction with an impersonal "government," acquires a relish for the word "bureaucrat" which it is not difficult to understand. But the President of the United States is also an elected official. He is, as Woodrow Wilson once tried to explain to a foreign diplomat, bound to be the interpreter of the great majority of the Ameri-can people, his duty being to divine the moment when the country requires action and to take that action which the great majority demands. During this period President Roosevelt has not deviated from his course or altered the essential policies on which the operations of the Government have been set.

Whatever the state of popular opinion may be when tested by specific issues, it is clear enough that the attack upon the "bureaucrats" was not without popular appeal. Men and women throughout the country were feeling the impact of total war in its progressively stronger pressure on the domestic front. The manpower barrel seemed almost empty, though we knew that it had not yet yielded nearly enough. The last stages of the conversion of industry from peace to war were being completed. Regulations and complicated restrictions seemed to multiply overnight. Could not the Government just issue a few simple orders and let the public, eager to further the grand effort, cooperate to the limit? Who was the Government to say what work was necessary for the war and what was not? What did the Government know about local conditions, about the needs of any particular locality, about the problems and the point of view of a minority group, about the urgent yet conflicting needs of farmers, of workers, of industrialists and consumers?

If this is what people were thinking, we have no cause for surprise. Add to this the frustration that all of us feel at not being able to do more to win the war. Our sons, our brothers or our husbands are fighting or may fight at any time, yet there is so little any one of us can accomplish to further the total effort, to lighten the burden they bear. Small wonder that we look for a whipping boy, and find him in that part of the Government that wears civilian clothes.

But after the whipping boy has been duly whipped we recognize, as indeed we must, that, as President Wilson wrote during the last war, "there is obviously but one instrumentality through which the war can be carried to a successful issue," and that instrumentality is the Government of the United States. Apart from the actual conduct of hostilities, the essential functions of the Government are and must necessarily be performed by civilian agencies, agencies which it is important to the country to keep in civilian hands.

III

You may say, I suppose, that I began by discounting Congressional criticism and now have put aside popular discontent, thus demonstrating in my own words that I qualify as a "bureaucrat." But if the test of a "bureaucrat" is either insensitivity to criticism or a belief in the infallibility of the Executive Branch, I cannot meet the test.

That there are weaknesses in the Executive Branch, its structure and organization and the occasional fragmentation of its authority, cannot be denied. That there are incompetent persons among the 2,943,919 employees shown in a recent enumeration is of course true. What is important is that the Government is essentially sound. For the Government of the United States today is not a party government. It is not a New Deal government. It is an aggregate of the best available civilian talent which this country can marshal, drawing upon persons who are not committed to activity in industry or agriculture or state or local government, no less necessary to be maintained than the work of the Federal Government itself. If that is so, a broad indictment of the personnel of the Government must necessarily fall to the ground. The largest single question that those who would expel the "bureaucrats" must ask themselves is, who is available to take their place? Viewed as anything more than change in the direction of government from the top, it is not a question to which, so far as I know, a satisfactory answer can be made.

The size of the Government has often been represented in grossly misleading terms. While the total personnel of almost three million has received great currency, it has not been adequately understood that approximately two thirds of this total, or about two million federal workers, are employed in the War and Navy Departments; principally, of course, in the arsenals, ship-yards, and other services of war production and supply. The remainder, of approximately a million employees, is about double the civilian personnel employed by the Federal Government (exclusive of the War and Navy Departments) in July, 1919. It is about 300,000 more than the total employees of the Government in 1933. And of the million employees outside the War and Navy Departments at the present time, 175,000 are employed in agencies exclusively devoted to the war; and 319,896 are employed in the Post Office, hardly a bureaucratic enterprise. In spite of this I do not say that the Government may not be overstaffed. Keeping in mind what has been done in the space of two short years to convert our productive capacities to the business of waging a total war, to exert the necessary controls over the domestic economy of 130,-000,000 people, to mobilize the national manpower, and to maintain the ordinary functions of government at the same time, it is natural that the instrumentalities developed for these purposes should prove not to be fool-proof. I say only that responsible criticism must take into account the magnitude of our achievement and the dimensions of the problems by which we have been faced.

Not the least of the problems confronted, and one that has by no means been overcome, is that of keeping the governmental organization together in the face of a constant drain upon its personnel. For employees of the civilian government, like those of private enterprise, have entered the armed services during the past two years at a constantly accelerating pace. As of December 1942, 26 per cent of the male personnel within the ages of 18 and 37 years had already entered the armed forces; a much larger percentage would necessarily obtain today. Yet charges were made and widely played up that the Government was a draft-evader's paradise, with occupational deferment the order of the day. On December 15, 1942, the President appointed a distinguished and disinterested committee composed of Paul Bellamy, Chairman, Eric Johnston and Ordway Tead to investigate the problem and formulate a general policy to govern the deferment of federal employees. The committee, in submitting its recommendations (since adopted by the President and approved by Congress), found that in the federal establishment

the extent of draft deferment has in the aggregate been moderate and conservative. A figure of slightly less than 2 per cent of the employees deferred is a good showing. It compares favorably with the experience of private industry in which a percentage figure of deferments at least twice as high is not deemed to be excessive and unwarranted.

The committee reported in February, 1943; its recommendations were adopted in an Executive Order issued by the President on March 6; the Report and the Order were transmitted to Congress on March 10; on March 17 the Senate Committee on Military Affairs reported favorably a bill to give explicit legislative approval to the Executive Order, and by early April the bill had become law. But at the same time that all this was taking place a subcommittee of the House Committee on Military Affairs undertook an examination of the deferment problem, with emphasis on individual cases; and the country was given the impression that the Executive Branch was guilty of wholesale evasion of the draft. Great publicity attended a finding that over 800,000 of the three million government employees are within the military service age, ignoring the fact that most of the individuals in question are husbands and fathers who have not yet been called up, with only an infinitesimal fraction deferred on occupational grounds.

I speak of the deferment problem at this length because it is important to take into account that the civil government as well as the armed services are engaged in fighting this war. I have in mind not only services performed by civilians directly related to military operations, such as the work of the Board of Economic Warfare and the War Production Board, and similar functions performed throughout the entire civil establishment. I mean to include any governmental service reasonably necessary in time of war. If such an essential activity collapses in the civilian branch it will necessarily be built up in the armed services, which quite properly will not hesitate to use personnel otherwise useful in the hostilities themselves. The Army and Navy now parallel much activity performed in civilian agencies. At the same time much of the skilled professional and administrative manpower that is being withdrawn from the civil government is employed in non-combatant work in the armed services inferior in importance to the work formerly done. If, as I believe, it is important to the country that civilian functions remain in civilian hands, there should not be military priority in such cases for obtaining civilian personnel. Functions should not be allocated between the military and civil branches only on the basis of a shortage of manpower produced by operation of the Selective Service Act. If experience on this score is necessary, we have but to turn to the British example, carefully contrived in this war to avoid the mistakes of the last.

IV

You will not understand by what I have said that I challenge the right and the duty of Congress—or for that matter of anyone else—to criticize and investigate the Government even in the midst of the war. The priority of Congress in matters of legislation and legislative policy is certainly not disputed by the Administration. The nature of the criticism and the extent of the investigation that can contribute to the attainment of our common goals are matters of honest judgment. Every investigation takes precious time from government officials, time otherwise devoted to the discharge of their normal duties and the administration of the war effort. It offers, in compensation for this loss, the valuable opportunity to set the groundwork for legislative action; to obtain legislative approval of what the Government is doing or attempting to do; to set the facts straight on the record, to clear the air of suspicion and recrimination, to advance the cause of public understanding at a time when it is needed most. Where there is suspected extravagance or negligence, a Congressional investigating committee can promptly and effectively lay bare the facts. The Truman Committee offers a striking example of this kind of work.

No one would defend the type of Congressional investigation symbolized, as Professor T. Harry Williams has recently reminded us, by the famous Committee on the Conduct of the War established at the end of 1861, because of the dissatisfaction of the Radicals with Lincoln's war aims and his conduct of the war. The Committee, consisting of three Senators and four Representatives, was granted broad powers to investigate "the general conduct of the war," past, present and future, and to summon persons and papers before it. As one Senator grimly put it, the purpose was to "probe the sore spots to the bottom." Executive sessions did not prevent news of what took place behind closed doors from finding its way into the press or into speeches on the floor of Congress. The Chairman, Senator Wade of Ohio, conceived of the Committee as giving Congress a voice in the war effort. As Professor Williams suggests: "The Committee was an experiment in civilian, Congressional control of the executive and the military in a democracy at war."

The experiment was not fortunate in its effect on the conduct of the war, over which it undoubtedly exercised great influence. The Committee tried to impose its inexpert knowledge of military affairs upon trained soldiers, with resulting confusion in direction and morale. Its approach was far too often partisan and biased. When, however, the Committee turned its attention to such problems as the production of war materials, its work, as Professor Williams points out, was often worth-while.

It is equally true, however, that the agencies of the Executive Branch can do much more than they have done to maintain adequate contact with the Congress, presenting through the medium of the standing committees the facts and the problems involved in administrative action with the fullness and continuity that cooperative effort demands. Some at least of the present controversy with respect to the exercise of delegated powers would never have arisen in any serious form if the Congress had felt itself adequately consulted in the flow of daily operations, and sufficiently informed. Let me illustrate by contrasting two recent experiences in legislative matters closely affecting the war.

The first, which typifies the executive-legislative relationship at its worst, is the history of the "Free Movement Bill," which proposed to empower the President to suspend for the duration of the war legislative restrictions on the free movement of property, persons and information required for the effective prosecution of the war. It was intended to speed up the whole war effort, and remove unnecessary delays, an obviously meritorious purpose. But the Administration—or more exactly that portion of the Administration interested in the passage of the bill —was not alive to its controversial aspects. The immigration laws, the customs laws, and the espionage laws have behind them long years of controversial history. The potentialities of political excitement were accentuated by the fact that the bill was introduced in the last days of the 77th Congress, when many defeated members were still sitting, and all were anxious to get home for a rest after an unusually long session. The stage was set for an explosion and the explosion came.

Those in charge of the bill did not take the trouble

47

to discuss it with the legislative leaders before causing it to be introduced. It was referred to the Ways and Means Committee, presumably on the ground that it involved the customs laws, although the members of the Immigration and Judiciary Committees would probably have been more familiar with the problems involved. The members of the Ways and Means Committee did not have the sense of participation in the proposed legislation which would have resulted from prior informal discussion or from carefully planned hearings. Had such discussion taken place there is little doubt that the broad powers which the bill purported to confer on the President could have been so modified as to make it obvious that no fundamental changes were being requested; and the ensuing violent opposition to the bill might have been forestalled.

The basis of the attack was that the immigration restrictions were being opened wide. What would prevent the admission to this country, under the excuse of war necessity, of hundreds of thousands of immigrants beyond the quotas fixed by law? Abuse of executive power, undermining our institutions, government by executive order—these charges raised such fury that it was then too late for the proponents of the bill to suggest, as they did, that they would readily agree to a clause providing that nothing in the bill should affect existing quotas.

It would be difficult to find a more striking example of failure of the legislative and executive branches to participate to a common end. Yet the result was unnecessary. The bill involved no genuinely controversial issues, or at least would not have involved them if the problem had been presented to Congress by the executive authorities in terms which afforded an adequate opportunity, prior to the public hearings, to achieve a cooperative solution of the actual problem at hand.

The legislative extension of the Lend-Lease Act by the new Congress, a measure of incalculable importance to the conduct of the war, presented a very different picture. In the two months before the bill was introduced, detailed discussion was held with legislative leaders and the Committee chairmen. Their judgment was obtained in advance on whether the extension should be for one year or a longer period, on the timing of the bill, and its relationship in time to the Lend-Lease Appropriation Act; and on various substantive features. Prior to this discussion, seven public reports had been made to Congress on the operations under the Act, and, shortly after the new Congress had convened, a special report was submitted covering the full program. A detailed and frank disclosure was made of the whole program during the hearings. The questions of Committee members were answered directly and promptly. As a result they felt that they were—as indeed they were —receiving genuine and candid assistance in discharging their legislative responsibility with respect to this unique and, in a sense, experimental legislation.

Some of the Republican members of the House Foreign Affairs Committee felt, for example, that Lend-Lease should be extended for two years rather than one. The Administration took the position that an extension for a year would suffice, that Congress should watch the operation, and, they felt confident, would extend it again if it proved satisfactory. How could the reaction of Congress be otherwise than sympathetic to such an approach? Another minority member of the Committee proposed an amendment to the Committee report, which was unanimously accepted, praising the Lend-Lease Administrator and his staff for their work in carrying on the Lend-Lease program. The vote in the House in favor of the bill was 407 to 6; in the Senate 82 to 0—in spite of the fact that, a few months before, there was evidence that there might be bitter political opposition to the bill when introduced. When Congress knew the facts and understood the importance and success of the program, it acted promptly and sympathetically to approve and extend it. Incidentally, the country was educated, and the mistaken impression that we were depriving ourselves of needed goods without any *quid pro quo* quickly disappeared. The bill was signed by the President on the same day that it was passed by the Senate—the second anniversary of the passage of the original Act.

The history of the bill shows what can be accomplished, even in moments of tension, by careful planning between the two branches, advance discussion, complete disclosure, adequate deference to the responsibility of Congress and hearings which are carefully prepared. The kind of relationship typified by this experience should be attainable in many fields. Reliance by Congress on the great standing committees and responsive development by the Executive Branch of the possibilities of cooperative effort should go a long way towards relieving the tension which has recently characterized the Washington scene. Substantive differences will, to be sure, remain. But the Government of the United States transcends any particular policies, and is not the property of a political group, whether the party in office or the opposition. What is of abiding importance to the conduct of the war is that the area of tension between the Congress and the Executive be reduced to minimal terms.

v

The Government's domestic war program is comparatively simple in outline. To attain maximum production of arms and essential products; to insure a wisely balanced distribution of manpower; to keep men at work by mechanisms which assure both management and labor a fair solution of their conflicting interests; to allocate scarce materials among the various needs—military and civilian, foreign and domestic—competing for consideration; to control prices, wages and profits and thus, without inequity to any of the interested groups, hold off the terrible threat of inflation—these are the fundamental objectives that our Government or, for that matter, any government in time of total war must pursue. The complications inhere in the procedures designed to achieve the objectives and the obvious difficulties of executing policies so all-embracing in scope. To us total war is a new experience, requiring above all things an informed and serious public opinion. Those who undertake to guide public opinion in these matters owe, at the very least, a duty to recognize accomplishments as well as to point out mistakes.

The country has been turned to war production at a strikingly increasing pace. A magnificent army has been built up, splendidly trained, well-equipped. Our great navy, with constant additions turned out far ahead of schedule, has shown what it can do in the Pacific without weakening the convoy of men and munitions to all parts of the world. Strikes have been held at a minimum. Public order has not been threatened, and civilian institutions have been maintained. While the cost of living has increased in this period of enormous expansion, unprecedented in the history of the world, the increase has not been dangerously extensive if we prove able to hold the line. These are the achievements of no single group—management, labor, government and the people everywhere have pulled together. Certainly the results do not indicate that any sweeping criticism of government, which conceived and directed the program, is justified by the facts.

I am tempted, therefore, to think that we are in a transitional stage of the war. Immediately after Pearl Harbor politics were pigeon-holed (it was said for the duration), the President got everything he asked for, Congress and the States did not oppose but insisted on comprehensive executive action. But then the manpower pinch was not felt; food was plentiful; inflation had only begun to look over the horizon. Today we are in the middle period, the period of irritation, of revolt against the inevitable change in our standards of living, necessary if we are to win, of criticism levelled at every mistake, however unavoidable. The air is full of charges and counter-charges, so that sometimes we wonder where the war is being waged. The third stage of the war has not yet begun. I mean the period when we shall have learned to accept the controls we have imposed on ourselves. It will take time to rectify our mistakes, to integrate the different programs, to have them understood and adopted. Such a unity has been achieved in England, but only after several years of experience of war. This is a larger country, younger and therefore with a shorter national tradition, with mixed bloods, greater in population as in territory. Yet what we have done in the last year encourages the thought that the problems which seem so difficult now will prove soluble before very long, that the final great effort will find us united and determined, not only to win—that we are—but to forego the recriminations and the squabbles that sap our strength and consume our time.

Only when we have reached this final stage of concerted effort shall we fully perform our duties to our country and our cause. For, as Woodrow Wilson reminded us, speaking on a May evening twenty-five years ago, we have two duties:

The first duty is to win the war. The second duty, that goes hand in hand with it, is to win it greatly and worthily, showing the real quality of our power not only, but the real quality of our purpose and of ourselves. . . .